CONTENTS

The Fireside Book

A picture and a poem for every mood
chosen by

David Hope

Printed and published by D.C. THOMSON & CO., LTD.,
185 Fleet Street, LONDON EC4A 2HS. © D.C. Thomson & Co., Ltd., 2010

JENNY

CHEERFUL little Jenny Wren,
 So small, so bright of eye,
A round, brown-feathered ball of fluff,
With perky tail cocked high.
She hops along the woody hedge,
She scavenges for food,
She builds her nest in tiny cracks
To raise her fledgling brood.
She never flees her homeland
But braves its Winter's chill,
Yet when the Spring comes calling
Just hear her joyful trill!

Margaret Ingall

8

HALLOWED HOUR

THE quiet light of evening
Has cast its golden glow,
Across the hills and valleys
Where gentle breezes blow.
A distant bird is calling
As rooks take homeward flight
Their shapes stand out in silhouette
Against the fading light.

The moon appears and sheds its beams
In twilight's darkening sky,
Just like a silver sickle
Suspended way up high.
There is a sense of stillness
In burrow, hedge and nest —
A quiet peace steals over all
This hallowed hour of rest.

Kathleen Gillum

HORSEMEN

THE white winged horsemen of the sea
  Their restless steeds command,
And wave on wave of cavalry
Go riding up the sand.

Swift as the tide of battle flows
They eagerly advance,
See how the warriors toss their plumes
The foaming chargers prance.

Beneath the rocky battlement
In placid pools they lie,
Their streaming crests in splendour spent
Time's mirrored pageantry.

But still upon the ceaseless shore
The phantom horsemen ride,
And all the chivalry of yore
Is echoed in the tide.

Edward Borland Ramsay

RAIN OR SHINE

THEY make a colourful display,
Even on a rainy day,
Vivid shades that seem to vie,
With the dark clouds in the sky,
Thro' all the ups and all the downs,
Both in countryside and towns,
Some held high whilst others low,
Turning white beneath the snow,
Umbrellas that are made
To keep us dry or in the shade.

12   *Brian H. Gent*

13

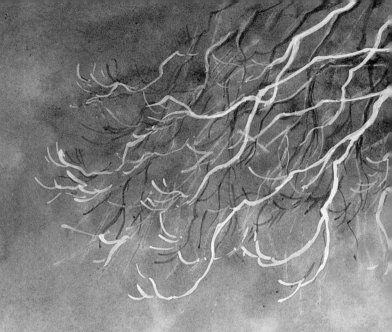

BENEATH THE BIRCHES

SLENDER silver trunks,
Thin branches, still devoid of leaf
Yet etched in lace against a pewter sky.
Later, frail buds will proffer
Tender wisps of greenery,
The first soft promise of leaves.
Now they stand in waiting,
But round their feet clusters of crocuses
Spill gold against new grass.
Purple and white add contrast to the gilded cups.
A speckled sampler, stitched by Spring.

Joan Howes

14

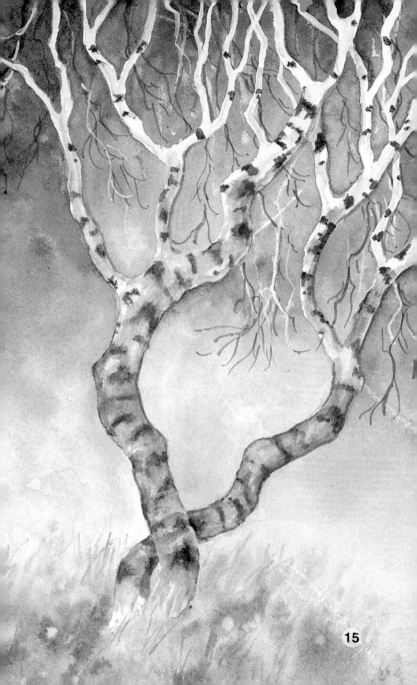

16

A VIEW AT MIDNIGHT

I MUSE upon the view that lies
Among the clouds in midnight skies;
Among the moon's pale yellow bars
And company of twinkling stars;
And in my quiet reverie
I see a charming tapestry —
A work of art which seems to hold
A blessedness in every fold,
And softly hung without a frame,
Without a great creator's name;
A glowing masterpiece to grace
The corridors of outer space.

Alice Jean Don

THE WIND

GIVE me the wind, a blustery day,
To blow all my sadness and sorrow away.
Give me the wind, as free as a bird,
That's blowing and gusting all over the world!
Give me the wind when I'm ready to roam,
A friend at my side till I wander back home.
Give me a wind that's blowing the leaves,
I know of no days that are better than these.
Give me a wind as I walk by the sea,
Moving the waves, that tells me I'm free.
Give me the wind, so faithful and true,
The best of companions that I ever knew.

Peter Cardwell

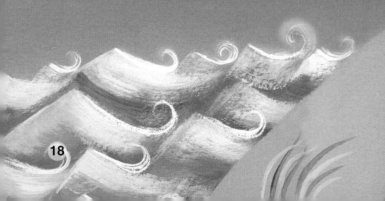

NEW SOUND

WE stopped and searched,
Listened and looked,
Scanned the branches,
Sifting oak and elm
For the source of sound
New to our ears.

No familiar blackbird flute,
Nor machine-gun magpie chatter;
No drum roll tapped
By distant woodpecker,
Nor song thrush tune
Pressed on repeat.

This time a simple
Penny-whistle trill,
Offered to all
To celebrate Spring,
In the way a nuthatch
Knows best.

David Elder

CASTLE IN SPAIN

WITH a promise I'll tease you,
I hope it will please you;
I've said it before but I'll say it again,
That I'll never forsake you,
And one day I'll take you
To live in my castle, my castle in Spain.

When the sun's warmly beaming,
Or the golden moon's gleaming,
How grandly it rises beyond a wide plain.
Hear trumpets blare loudly,
See banners stream proudly,
To welcome us both to my castle in Spain.

All right, it's a dream, dear,
A sweet foolish scheme, dear,
And really I know that I'm dreaming in vain;
But I see it so clearly,
I love it so dearly,
My castle, my very own castle in Spain.

Peter Cliffe

MINING SUNLIGHT

SUN bores through a seam of dense cloud
until it reaches sea, drills through ice-blue water,
filling the hole with so much gold
it overflows, an ever-widening puddle
that slowly sinks and drains
as the sides cave in under the force of cumulus.

Wind is a blunt chisel, chipping the waves,
revealing striations that glitter with pyrites,
their false promise soon buried beneath
shale shadows that clog the surface.

Sunset dribbles from a crack in the cloud face,
then gushes in a copper spray
that twists and coils as if alive,
before seeping away, its power spent.

The watcher is left to prospect for opalescent light,
last twists of apricot and rose flickering against the blue
that deepens slowly to coal.

Rowena M. Love

HAWTHORNS

WHAT pure delight
when they first took
our breath away
on that May sighting,
when for a while
bursting with freshness
they looked their best,
gave their all,
day upon day a sheer
white snowflake lustre.
Then came a pouring
spiral and spin,

a bridal thaw as
these two months marrie
and a cruel wind blew
and clusters of petals
fuelled by its shake
flew like confetti,
frail as moths,
delighting us again
with the palest petticoat
train, floating in the wake
of June's new sandals.

John Ellis

ERRATIC,
RANNOCH MOOR

HERE again a boulder,
Grey-granite grounded,
Left lying long ago
By the slow train of ice
That crept unnoticed
In standing-still time.

Only the melt-water,
Confident in its clarity,
Ever knew the secret
Of the journey taken,
Whispering the myths
Of an uplands birth.

And here it's been
Ever since,
Orphaned and alone,
Waiting to be adopted
By some new, unimagined
Mother of ice.

David Elder

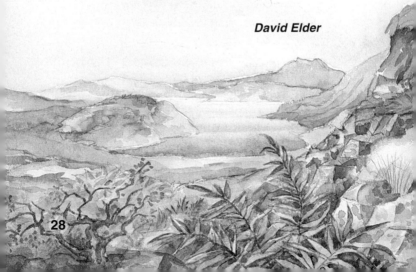

A BRIEF VERSE OF SUMMER

BETWEEN the lines of March and May
I read a verse that seemed to say,
with flowery words upon the page,
that Summer's young and bashful stage
had come with the desire to stay.
For who would wonder otherwise?
The crocuses gave glad advice
to churlish winds that spoke of snow —
to gather up their gales and go,
giving leaf and bloom reprise.
But May had not made up its mind
and scheming squalls were swift to find
an incomplete account of Spring,
and marked with wintry silvering
where Nature's hand forgot to sign.

Rachel Wallace-Oberle

CRESTED TIT

NO, not like the guide book says,
Black and white with grey-brown black,
But, in the Summer sunset light,
Awash with gold and rose-tinged beige,
The crested tit at pinewood edge
Sits, then hops, swaps branch
For branch on caterpillar trail
And, in the crevices, searches
For aphid, berry, seed,
Until the sun goes down
And, undulating back to forest heart,
It finds a secret hole
No one can find.

David Elder

33

FORGET-ME-NOTS

THE lilac was soon over,
now the May rain
cries out for Summer.

Grassy limbs reach up,
raindrops fill the buttercup,
and the pale bluebell
wrings with wet.

Leaves of the dog-rose
skilfully bear,
like prized oysters,
pearls of water.

The dandelion sheds
its mane of grey,
forget-me-nots remind
of another May.

John Ellis

SUMMER GOLD

NOW soft May days give place to florid June
And Spring's pale pastels burn more bright and bold.
Laburnum's yellow hair lifts in the breeze,
The meadows wear a crown of summer gold.

With Midas fingers nature gilds the scene,
Scattering buttercups in careless drifts.
Each daisy-heart glows like a topaz stone
And June is surfeit with shining gifts.

Joan Howes

JUST FOR A DAY

OUT of a wrinkled chrysalis,
  Suddenly you've come to this,
Your fairy wings are sheer delight,
That give you fleeting, flitting flight,
You while away the Summer hours,
Calling on the upturned flowers,
To spend your whole life in the sun,
Until your span on earth is spun.
If only I could find a way,
To fly with you for just one day . . .

Brian H. Gent

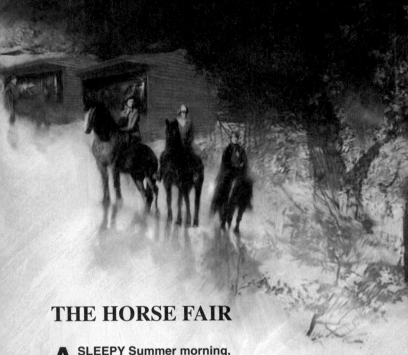

THE HORSE FAIR

A SLEEPY Summer morning,
A stirring in the breeze,
The distant clip of horses,
Bright colours glimpsed through trees.
And now they're coming closer.
Their vardos rumbling near,
The men, the girls, the children,
The travelling folk are here.
And soon the town is humming
Alive with cheerful sound,
With bartering and banter,
And hooves on cobbled ground.
They will not stay forever,
They'll soon be gone for sure,
Yet just for now — enjoy it,
It's Horse Fair Week once more!

Margaret Ingall.

WILD IRISES

A GALE of children swept in today
With wild bunches of flowers.
They left them laughing on the kitchen table
And in a gust were gone.

All day they ran themselves free
Up hills and down;
At seven they came home, blown out,
Sunset burning their faces.

Now the house is fast asleep;
It leans into the wind, smoke
Hurrying at an angle from chimney —
The flowers on the table shining.

Kenneth Steven

JULY AWAKENING

BATHED in blue
The morning breaks open,
Its busy-ness
Held in check
Like the bumble bee
Trapped inside,
Bumping, bouncing
Off the clear sash
Window pane.

A pigeon coos
A quiet quatrain
Down the chimney
Of fireside sleep,
Wooing us back to bed,
But not before the swifts
Counter in chorus
Their urgent refrain
Awake! Awake!

Now at last
The bee picks the spot,
Finding the open gap,
Out into the infinite air
It revs, then throttles
Off, all cylinders
blazing,
Going through the gears,
As if making up
For lost time.

David Elder

SUMMER THOUGHTS

TRAFFIC passing, children playing,
Distant music on the air,
Sounds of Summer, gently flowing,
Thoughts of you grow everywhere.
Memories of other Summers,
Sunlit meadow, rain-washed street,
Early morning by the river
When the air was fresh and sweet.

Love that chased away the shadows,
Brought the sunshine after rain,
Thoughts of Summer may be fading,
Thoughts of you will still remain.
Sudden storms and Summer lightning,
Weather changing, like our lives,
Blossom falls and flowers wither,
Love is endless, love survives.

Iris Hesselden

ONCE IN A SUNLIT MEADOW

ACROSS the grassy meadow sweet
　　where bluets toss their blooms in praise,
where breezes climb the steepled heat,
and hymns upon the wing are raised;
there purple spires of thistle heads
kneel as finch and thrush align
to contemplate and leave unsaid
my silent trespass in their shrine.

Rachel Wallace-Oberle

50

AFTERNOON TEA

HAZY Summer afternoons,
  Tinkling teacups, silver spoons,
Lettuce sandwiches in squares,
Plaited wicker basket chairs,
Conversation, laughter, too,
Under skies of azure blue,
Grandma 'neath a parasol,
Sister with her china doll,
Father smiling, pipe aglow,
Our Labrador with pups in tow.
Mother there to organise,
Pour the tea and supervise,
Lemonade and ginger pop,
Dundee cake with nuts on top,
Strawberries and clotted cream,
Lazy days in which to dream;
Alas it's all so long ago,
Yet happy memories still flow
Of when my family and me,
Gathered on the lawn for tea.

Brian H. Gent

GOLDEN DREAMS

HEAVEN'S jewelling
   And all is blue skies and sunshine
gilding the rock pools.
The seaweed garlands and green moss
a sapphire emerald and rose hue
reflected in the flux of sparkling water.
Spume sallies back and forth and
collars the cream peach shore.
Adventure caves, the net fishing and the
Olympics of surfboarding jellyfish.
There's gloss of tangerine gold on the high seas
And the shrill lament of a seagull hovering
to catch a scrap of chip.
With more dissolving castles to build
the youngsters chase the sea till teatime
and all is blue skies and sunshine gold.

52   *Dorothy McGregor*

FOXGLOVES

IN shaded, secret glens
  They build their spires,
Long — sleek — straight,
Seeking the divine,
Everlasting light.

There, under stillness
By day and night,
They fasten bells
Forged, hand-crafted,
Smoothed by silk.

Until, one by one,
They drop in turn —
Moments of Spring
Lost in the undergrowth
Of the circling year.

David Elder

55

CROW ON THE BEACH

YOU held your own against
The motley array of grey, white and speckled birds
Pecking and arguing on the shore.
Imperious as a barrister,
You gleamed like jet against
The muted gold of sand.
Scorning the raucous squawks
And squabbles of the gulls,
You stepped primly among the stones,
Your beak a shining ebony dagger
Probing for morsels amidst
Spent shells and bladderwrack.
When the gulls flapped noisily out to sea
You spread your sable wings
And with a departing caw,
Rose higher and higher
To reach the green sanctuary of tall trees.

Joan Howes

THE BIRDS IN MY GARDEN

I'VE watched the birds at Summer long
fill my garden with their song;
among the pansy, rose and phlox,
composing sonnets with their talk
of golden days and verdant trees,
they've quietly made me believe
that Nature's most enchanting words
are spoken in the grace of birds.

Rachel Wallace-Oberle

HARPS

THEY came from lands afar,
Older than Stonehenge,
Harps, lyres, tensioned strings
Of brass and braided bronze,
Gracing their art in shape and sound
From Luxor to Nepal,
Tumbling tunes, trickling streams,
Through Tara's ancient halls.

Don Robinson

61

GLORY

WHEN wild grape and tangled woodbine fade
and fields lie darkly churned beneath the blade,
when withered weed and aster spice the air,
I walk up through their solemn Autumn prayer
and wonder at the fragile magic there.

High above the russet-coloured trees
that cling with ardour to reluctant leaves,
the sudden bittersweet farewell of birds
calls to me in melancholy words
that still my heart yet leave it strangely stirred.

I linger on the empty garden path
and deeply drink of Summer's aftermath
and crush the last pale roses to my breast,
dreaming of the fragrance of their breath —
on every side by quiet glory pressed.

Rachel Wallace-Oberle

A DREAM OF DOLPHINS

LAST night I dreamed of dolphins,
   of dolphins wild and free,
who plunged through crystal waters,
who owned the silver sea.
And I was swimming with them,
accepted by their side,
as playmate and an equal,
we leaped the oceans wide.
And on we raced together,
so effortless and strong,
I shared their exultation,
I joined their primal song.
Too soon, as dawn came creeping,
my dream dissolved away,
Yet still that joy, that gladness
remains with me today.

Margaret Ingall

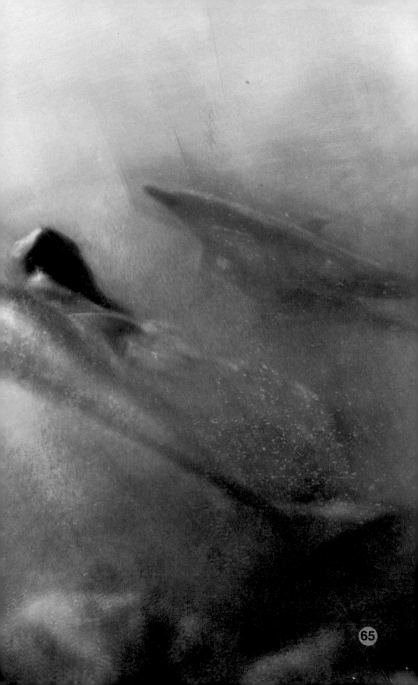

GREY DAY

SLATES rattle as wind whips round eaves,
   drowning out sound
of alabaster gulls
pinned to the day
like a lepidopterist's display.

Clouds scud haematite swirls
across silver sky.
They bunch and fold
from voile to velvet
trailing their marabou trim
of heavy rain.

Gorse clings iron filings
to a headland dithered by the squall.
Far below cliffs darkened to charcoal,
pewter sea gouged with white horses
pounds at the shore.

Rowena M. Love

67

AVOCET

COVET a bird,
A cryptic clue, maybe,
Feathered fandangos of courtship
Near the Suffolk sea.
A meagre nest,
A scrape in the mud,
Eggs set snug and warm;
Pools of sweet and salty shrimp
Nourishing newly-born.

Snowy white, a yelping cry,
A slender upturned beak;
Blue legs trailing long and thin
Above those shifting creeks.

Don Robinson

WHEN SUMMER GOES GENTLY

WHEN geese cry overhead
from sombre skies that lurch with toppled cloud,
when the trill is stilled of a hundred tiny birds
who hold twilight parties in my garden,
when rose and birch weep on my lawn,
when dawn ties frosted knots around each blade of grass,
I know Summer has gone gently
and an aching wonder sidles through my heart.
But my upturned spirit searches,
breathlessly,
for a timid sun tangled in treetops,
for new stars piercing through,
for Autumn's spices on the wind
and whispers, without regret,
with fondness,
"Farewell."

Rachel Wallace-Oberle

HARVEST TIME

I WALKED along the path
Past "Unprotected cliff edge" signs,
Following the coast line north,
First glancing left at the combines,
Taking their turn to stop,
Start, and change direction,
Transforming the fields to stripes;
And then looking right at the fishing boats
Side-stepping the rocks,
Treading water to gather in creels.
At August end a harvest time
For land and sea.

David Elder

73

SWEET MEMORIES

I CLOSE my eyes and ruminate,
And see a boy go thro' a gate,
Up the road, right to the top,
To that magic corner shop,
Where with a penny in your hand,
You held the key to wonderland,
The bell that tinkled on a coil,
And door that squeaked devoid of oil,
What a sight there met the eyes,
In this sweetmeat enterprise,
Sherbet dabs and lemon drops,
Liquorice sticks and soda pops,
Lettered rock and toffee bars,
On shelves that reached up to the stars,
An Eldorado, Shangri-la,
A feast of gems in every jar,
And tho' it was so long ago,
Sweet memories still come and go,
For when I close my eyes I see,
That little boy who once was me . . .

Brian H. Gent

75

AN OLD BATTLEFIELD

THE evening broods; it's growing late;
I lean upon a mossy gate
To watch the deep-blue leave the sky,
And see the homing rooks drift by.

They say that men came here to fight,
But not who won, whom put to flight.
The battle raged so long ago,
And why 'twas fought we'll never know.

Beyond the shadows of the trees
The lush grass ripples in the breeze.
The sun slips down behind the hill,
And all is restful, hushed and still.

Then, half a-dream, I seem to hear,
Faint and afar, but ringing clear,
The war-horns of a coming throng,
Eager for combat, right or wrong.

Peter Cliffe

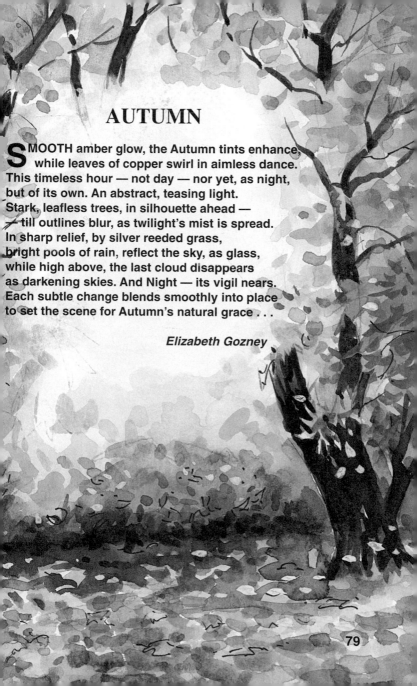

AUTUMN

SMOOTH amber glow, the Autumn tints enhance,
 while leaves of copper swirl in aimless dance.
This timeless hour — not day — nor yet, as night,
but of its own. An abstract, teasing light.
Stark, leafless trees, in silhouette ahead —
till outlines blur, as twilight's mist is spread.
In sharp relief, by silver reeded grass,
bright pools of rain, reflect the sky, as glass,
while high above, the last cloud disappears
as darkening skies. And Night — its vigil nears.
Each subtle change blends smoothly into place
to set the scene for Autumn's natural grace . . .

Elizabeth Gozney

79

WIND DANCER

IT must be fine to be a crow,
to wing on watery flight
or on the warm sirocco,
not to mind the chill wind's bite
nor suffer from vertigo.

To be such a devil-may-care,
rollicking, frolicking acrobat,
revelling daily there
on gentle breeze or furious draught,
playing aerial solitaire.

Dark as a thundercloud,
buzzard chasing, chancing alone
or with a harassing crowd,
compere to all, fearful of none,
boisterous, bold and loud.

John Ellis

SUNDAE SUNSET

FLYING home to Abbotsinch,
chill Sunday serves up
a taste of Summer fruit
when strawberry sun sinks
in a generous scoop of scarlet.

Beneath blueberry clouds,
thick layer of apricot
oozes sweetness along the horizon,
melting into lemon sorbet
tart as the November air.

Dusk serves up the Clyde,
spreading its chocolate sauce
in a lazy swirl flicked
with nautical vermicelli.

A flaked almond moon garnishes the sky,
above the skoosh of snow
that creams Goatfell and Ben Lomond,
while far below city neon
sprinkles hundreds and thousands
across the airport approach.

Rowena M. Love

THROUGH RAIN-FILLED WOODS

I BRIEFLY stopped for shelter, unconcerned,
beneath a beech that quivered, water-stained,
beside the goldenrod and wild fern
and watched the quiet woods fill up with rain.

The birds said less from high within the trees,
as leaf and limb were sluiced until they shone;
there, below green, tossing canopies
I paused until the last dark clouds were gone.

And when the sun admonished grass to stand
and resurrected lilies pale as bone,
conversation in the woods began
and I, unwilling, found the footpath home.

Rachel Wallace-Oberle

THE QUINCES

THAT Autumn we stayed in an old manse;
A place full of ticking clocks that sounded
Like disapproving Victorian gentlemen.

At breakfast between a hurry of bowls and courses
She told us of the laden trees in the garden,
All these quinces she hadn't time to pick.

Late that afternoon I went out
Under the blue-cold skies of October
A world closed in by trees and crows.

A low sun pierced the woods in a bonfire of light;
All round the house the lanes
Were gullies of red and gold leaves.

But that garden was yellow-white globes on branches
The colour of mistletoe berries, lamps of things
Shaped like pears.

Their stalks broke like ice,
Cracked in the frozen stillness —
I put them, piece by piece, in a basket.

I went back, wondering what her kitchen would smell like —
What things it would make for the Winter —
The quince frothing in pans like lava.

Kenneth Steven

LITTLE THINGS

ISN'T it a wondrous thing,
   How fragile little mem'ries cling,
Incidents that were so small,
You think time never could recall,
The "blueness" of a cloudless sky,
Tireless swallows flitting by,
Heady scents of briar roses,
Meadow flowers meant for posies,
Grandma darning grandad's sock,
The chiming of the mantle clock,
And when the fire embers glowed,
Toasting crumpets a la mode,
The magic when the dawn sun glints,
On browns and reds of Autumn tints,
Cards and presents, wine that's mulled,
Crackers waiting to be pulled,
That special feeling of good cheer,
Togetherness with those held dear,
What further evidence could mount,
To prove it's little things that count . . .

Brian H. Gent

CITY OAK

I PASSED it every day
But had not noticed
The power of its presence
Standing tall, broad,
Gnarled and wrinkled,
A beacon of steadfastness
Usually dimmed in neon world,
Yet today lit up
By absent volts.
And a bright shroud of fog.

Its electric force
Charged the November air
And my daily commute
Changed for evermore.

David Elder

91

CRUMBS OF COMFORT

WHEN earth becomes as hard as nails
   And Winter's steely grip prevails
So thro' this petrified façade
Access to sustenance is barred
Small wonder sparrows look forlorn
On an icing sugared lawn
Robins, blackbirds, thrushes, too
Are captured by the Arctic brew
So every time that Jack Frost comes
I take a tray of crusty crumbs
And place them on a garden seat
As a special daily treat
Crumbs of comfort for my friends
Till unrelenting Winter ends . . .

Brian H. Gent

EAST SANDS

WINTER slammed in hard that night.
Rain battered my windows, thrumm
and tap danced along the glass roof,
wrenched open the shed door.
I had seen the signs driving home:

cauliflower clouds massed
in a phosphorescent sky,
the Newport houses brittle white
against the Tay's lurid, steely grey.
The sea roared all the next day —

94

here was no let up here, at the East Sands.
Logs and planks bobbed lopsidedly
n the silt-brown burn. The town
vas sea-washed, empty. Then,
miracle, an Autumn swansong,

when the mist rose to reveal the sun.
A few russet leaves still clung, pinned to the trees;
he sea stayed huge for several days.
Tonight, a ring of frost encircles the moon.

Ruth Walker

MOONLIGHT

THE velvet curtain of the sky
  Is pierced with shafts of light,
As moonbeams stretch their silver streamers
Out into the night.
Falling on the sleeping fields
The earth is bathed below
With images of light and shade
Which give an eerie glow.

The trembling leaves of midnight trees
Which breezes bend and sway,
Look like shining, silken shapes
Where shadows dance and play.
Sending down her radiant beams
All streaming from on high,
The moon looks like a silver lamp
Suspended in the sky.

Kathleen Gillum

97

A BASKET OF KITTENS

WITH laundry neatly stowed away
In dresser, chest and drawer,
Upon the old clothes basket
Comes a cautious, snowy paw;
Then from her jaws, the mother cat
Lays down a tiny kitten —
Bold ginger stripes upon its back,
Snow-white, each little mitten.

Away from Winter's icy blast,
The little mother stows
Each precious one with loving care —
The old range warmly glows.
With happy purrs she tends their needs
And feeds each tiny mite;
Then, Mama Pusskin curling round —
They're tucked in for the night!

Maggie Smith

100

SUN-SHIVER

WILLOWS were brushed with gold
   And ancient beeches gloried in their flames.
An unexpected sun banished November's gloom,
Dispelling hints of Winter's icy claims.

Berries burned brightly through a trove of leaves,
Touched by the season's Midas fingertips.
A few remaining blackberries stayed fast,
Dusky temptation staining hands and lips.

Yet presage underscored the brilliance,
A sudden wind bore breath of later snows.
Shivers released the few remaining leaves —
Against the wall a Winter jasmine glowed.

Joan Howes

NATURE'S NIGHTLY PLAY

A FLECK of moon in a charcoal sky,
The screech as a tawny owl flies by,
Bats emerge on silent wings,
From lofted caves by mountain springs,
Badgers take their timid amble,
Foraging round hedge and bramble;
Whilst out of holes peer furry heads,
To sniff the air by flower beds,
And purposefully shell-topped snails,
Glide and leave their pearlised trails,
So staged is nature's nightly play,
Until there breaks another day . . .

Brian H. Gent

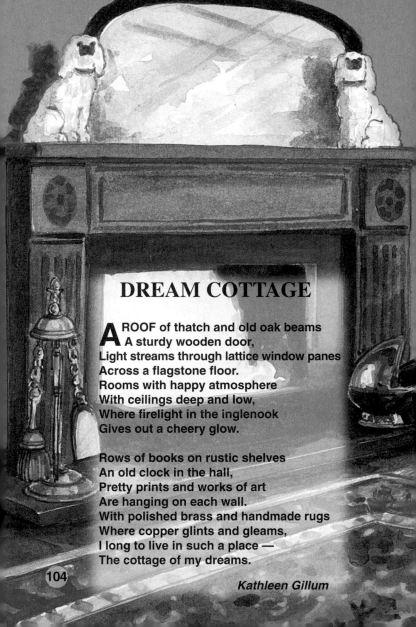

DREAM COTTAGE

A ROOF of thatch and old oak beams
A sturdy wooden door,
Light streams through lattice window panes
Across a flagstone floor.
Rooms with happy atmosphere
With ceilings deep and low,
Where firelight in the inglenook
Gives out a cheery glow.

Rows of books on rustic shelves
An old clock in the hall,
Pretty prints and works of art
Are hanging on each wall.
With polished brass and handmade rugs
Where copper glints and gleams,
I long to live in such a place —
The cottage of my dreams.

Kathleen Gillum

FROZEN IN TIME

BY frozen lake
and frosted lawn,
Pale shines the sun
on Winter's dawn.
Tenacious cling
the beech tree leaves,
As icicles cascade
from eaves.
Blackened twines
the fruitless thorn,
Once vibrant borders
now forlorn.

Snowflakes gently
flutter down,
Cloaking countryside
and town.
There is no movement,
all is still,
Bending to
the frozen will.
Until in coppice,
wood and lane,
Brave little snowdrops
bloom again.

Brian H. Gent

BY STARLIGHT

I'VE seen by starlight onyx skies that flow
and hurl their waves upon a moonlit shore;
endless midnight seas that toss and blow
cleansing Heaven's alabaster floor.

I've seen by starlight soundless trees that stand
assembled into shadowed turrets tall;
nocturnal castles built by spectral hands
that haunt the gloom with dim, enchanted walls.

I've seen by starlight mirrored rivers gleam;
silver cords that tether field and hill,
brimming with the moon's diaphanous beams,
rushing by yet standing strangely still.

By starlight I have loved the darkened Earth
and walked with her across the pillared night,
as she drowses in her spangled berth
and dreams of wearing diamonds strung with light.

Rachel Wallace-Oberle

The artists are:-

TS Carmichael; Hallowed Hour.
Jackie Cartwright; Summer Thoughts,
Crow On The Beach, An Old Battlefield,
Dream Cottage.
John Dugan; Horsemen,
Erratic Rannoch Moor, Moonlight.
Harry McGregor; Afternoon Tea,
Sundae Sunset, City Oaks, East Sands,
Sun Shiver.
Keith Robson; Grey Day.
Maria Taylor; The Wind,
Nature's Nightly Play, By Starlight.
Ruth Walker; Mining Sunlight.
Joseph Watson; Hawthorns,
Crested Tit, Avocet,
When Summer Goes Gently,
Crumbs Of Comfort.
Staff Artists; Jenny, Rain Or Shine,
Beneath The Birches, A View At Midnight,
New Sound, Castle In Spain,
A Brief Verse Of Summer, Forget-Me-Nots,
Summer Gold, Just For A Day,
The Horse Fair, Wild Irises,
July Awakening, Once In A Sunlit Meadow,
Golden Dreams, Foxgloves,
The Birds In My Garden, Harps, Glory,
A Dream Of Dolphins, Harvest Time,
Sweet Memories, Autumn, Wind Dancer,
The Quinces, Through Rain-filled Woods,
Little Things, A Basket Of Kittens,
Frozen In Time.